ANTHOLOGY OF 25 POEMS AND LYRICS

Second Edition

ANTHOLOGY OF 25 POEMS AND LYRICS

Political Failure Poetry |
Love and Memories Poetry |
Lyrics

Bernard Bernie Heys MCMI. CIWFM. DipBs

To order additional copies of this book, contact:
Xlibris
UK TFN: 0800 0148620 (Toll Free inside the UK)
UK Local: (02) 0369 56328 (+44 20 3695 6328 from outside the UK)
www.Xlibrispublishing.co.uk
Orders@Xlibrispublishing.co.uk
859505

CONTENTS

Introduction vii

Fifth Project ix

Prime Charity xi

Author Background xiii

Mary Carmel Heys xv

Poems And Lyrics xxiii

1 When The Virus Struck 1

2 Ode To Carmel 4

3 Lockdown 9

4 Ode To George Floyd 10

5 The Viral Pimpernel 11

6 For The Welfare Of My Child 14

7 Ode To Radcliffe 16

8 Radcliffe On Irwell 19

9 It Is Your Moral Duty 22

10 Leadership Lost 25

11 The Year Democracy And Communities Died 28

12 The Party Of Law And Order 30

13 The House Of Cowards 32

14 Boris The Educated 35

15 If We Never Meet Again 38

16 Fun Was Fun When We Were Young 40

17 Empty Streets Of London 43

18 Please Don't Leave Me 44

19 Tears In Mt Heart 46

20 When We Were Young 49

21 Love Is In The Cloud 51

22 Poetry In Shielding Lyrics In Lockdown 52

23 If You Have The Gift Of Life 55

24 Missing You At Christmas 57

25 Lost Martha 59

Addendum A 63

Addendum B 65

Addendum C 69

Addendum D 77

Addendum E 83

Addendum F 85

Pre-Shielding 89

INTRODUCTION

Second Edition.

ANTHOLOGY OF 25 POEMS AND LYRICS
Political Failure Poetry Love and Memories Poetry
I have added Missing you at Christmas for Carmel. Lyrics.

Mary Carmel Heys Carmel's Corner. Ireland forever

We were not allowed to support you in your greatest hour of need by a self-serving government.

Her light shines on in those she loved. Her spirit lives in the morning hills the flowers and the trees.

Loving daughter, wife, mother, and friend to all she met in an extraordinary international life, dedicated to teaching children with special needs.

Bernard (Bernie) Heys MCMI. CIWFM. DipBs
www.theradcliffelad.co.uk.

Poetry in Shielding, Lyrics in Lockdown.

The Radcliffe Lad: 02.02.2020 to 25.12.2023

Anthology of 25 Satirical and Contemporary Poems and Lyrics. Including:

The Viral Pimpernel
The Welfare of my Child (Dominic Cummings)
Ode to George Floyd
Bernard (Bernie) Heys

The Radcliffe Lad Logo

FIFTH PROJECT

Www.theradcliffelad.co.uk
Fifth Publishing Project
"Invictus Maneo. My soul remains unconquered."

Preamble.:

This is the fifth publishing project, a "Print on Demand" Self-Publishing in-house Team effort of the Heys Family and orders will be fulfilled to an agreed lead time with our Printer who has advised on the technical preparation of the editing and formatting by Dr Michelle Heys, Editor in Chief. I trust that you will continue to support the very worthy cause as described for the Neotree for life Charity.

As with the first project this Anthology, "Poetry in Shielding" has been penned by the Author whilst on Dialysis three days per week in Skipton Renal Unit and my thanks to their excellent care.

Bernard (Bernie) Heys   *bernieheys@gmail.com*
01282 843073   07484246126   25.12.2023
theradcliffelad@gmail.com
www.theradcliffelad.co.uk

Web Architect Wisdom.
Bernard Heys MCMI., CWIFM. DipBs.

Please contact me by email and I will forward copy of the book description. To discuss please phone, noting that I am on dialysis Monday, Wednesday, Friday and not available on these days.
Hard copy Print on Demand.

Hard copies will be signed by the Author if requested.

Sales of the Hard-Back book will contribute £2.00 to support the Neotree Charity No 1186748 www.neotree.org
Attention Dr Michelle Heys. michelleheys@gmail.com
eBook: Amazon: Kindle version www.amazon.co.uk/Remember
Member OnlineBookClub.org   02.02.2020
Prime Charity: NeoTree.No1186748.

Pre-amble Our first project:
'Remember Radcliffe Lad Know Your Station In Life'
A life autobiography from 10 11.1939 to 10 11 2019
ISBN: 978-1-9133-15-1
ASIN: B0875MCW36

PRIME CHARITY

Dr Michelle Heys, PI NeoTree
Associate Professor UCL, UK and
Consultant Paediatrican and joint Associate
Clinical Director, East London NHS
Foundation Trust, UK
16th Jan 2020

On behalf of: the wider NeoTree team

On behalf of: the NeoTree team

www.neotree.org   #the_neotree   neotreeapp@gmail.com   @the_neotree

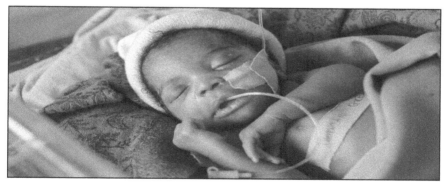

Every year OVER ONE MILLION babies die on their day of birth.

Seventy percent of new-born deaths are preventable by implementing low-cost solutions effectively and mobile technologies offer an avenue for implementation.

The Neo-Tree supports healthcare workers (HCWs) in delivering these solutions using a tablet-based application (app) to prompt

clinical actions, provide education, collect information about babies and feed data back to HCWs and national health systems.

Our overall vision is to use best practice and information technology to improve clinical decisions for new-born care and increase rates of new-born survival in under-resourced health care settings.

Dr Michelle Heys *www.neotree.org*
michelleheys@gmail.com
Author Bernard Heys *bernieheys@gmail.com*
Editor in Chief: Dr Michelle Heys
Web Advisor: James Heys. *jamesheys@gmail.com*
Marketing Advisor: Robert Heys. *rob_heys@hotmail.com*
theradcliffelad@gmail.com
www.theradcliffelad.co.uk

In Memory of all the victims of Covid19 -Sars.Cov2S COV2.
'Remember John Ruskin; The only wealth is life.'
The Radcliffe lad

AUTHOR BACKGROUND

Bernard Heys, born 10.11.1939, at Bealey Maternity Home Radcliffe Lancashire, to Walter and Martha Heys.

He was educated at both infant and junior level at St Mary's RC School and secondary at Thornleigh Salesian College Bolton to GCSE Level.

He continued his Further Technical education, to HNC level, at Radcliffe Technical College, Bolton Technical College and Hatfield Institute of Technology in Aeronautical and Mechanical Engineering Design, with further studies in Electrical Engineering, Mechanics of Fluids and Structures.

He obtained a Diploma in Business Studies from Alexander Hamilton Institute, when working with Kellogg International.

The first six years of his career were spent with De Havilland Aircraft Co Ltd followed by four years in the production business of high-speed special purpose plant and equipment for paper, textile, and hospital laundry and cable production.

The next eighteen years were spent on the management of mega projects in Aluminium Smelting, Ship Building, Oil, Gas and Petrochemicals, Oil Refining and Polypropylene Facilities, Steel Production, North Sea Oil Facilities, Dubai Dry Dock, Al Jubail Industrial City and Jeddah Waste- Water Treatment with Buwayb Riyadh Facilities.

The next four years were spent on a four year turn around -project for a multinational conglomerate with facilities in eighty countries.

Finally, twenty-five years running a business The Cranwood Partnership providing "Management, Technical and Consultancy Services for major blue-chip companies and public and private organisations pioneering the market in Facilities Management. During my working career I spent many years in volunteering activities and specialising as a BSI expert in the development of Harmonised Standards in Europe on a voluntary basis.

I retired at seventy-two through poor health.

This was the start of my formal fourth career of writing and publishing. Bernard Heys 10.11.2023

MARY CARMEL HEYS

Mary Carmel Sweeney:

Mary Carmel Sweeney was born in Bealey's maternity home, Radcliffe on 02.05.1942, the only child of Anne and Hugh Sweeney. Hugh Sweeney was a Baker by profession and was called up to serve in the Catering Corps during the war, afterwards returning to the Co-op Bakery in Radcliffe. Her mother Anne Kiernan had travelled from Edgeworth Town in County Longford Ireland in order to find work in the UK.

At that time in Ireland females were not considered to be in line to inherit the farm property owned by the family and accordingly the Kiernan farm succession was to Jimmy Kiernan, her brother.

Anne met and married Hugh Sweeney and initially lived in Egerton Street, directly opposite the gates of the very large Gas Works. Mary Carmel was baptized, made her first communion, and confirmed at St Mary's RC Church Radcliffe and attended St Mary's Infants and Junior School in Victoria Street and left school at 15.

She continued her skills training and domestic science plus City and Guilds courses in sewing and clothing production processes and as they lived in Egerton Street, Carmel then initially worked in the office of the gas works and later transferred to the sales office in Manchester and Bury.

Anne and Hugh would host other young ladies arriving from Ireland to find work and also to find husbands locally. Kathleen Duffy arrived and married Dennis Walsh at St Mary's and Danny

Boyles' mother Babs arrived and married Frank Boyle also in St Mary's. George and Eileen Watmough met and married in Belfast. All three families became life- long friends. All three couples were guests at our wedding in 1970.

Dennis and Kathleen Walsh had four children, Jeannette, Kathryn, Dianne and Brendan and their eldest daughter Janette became very good friends with Carmel. Dennis had studied engineering and specialized in Thermodynamics, especially steam and superheated steam for power generation. Initially he worked in the Gas Works laboratory and then moved into teaching eventually as senior lecturer at Burton Tech. We had much in common to discuss over the years on our visits to Burton, the center of brewing in the UK due to the special qualities of the water.

Frank and Babs Boyle had three children Danny, Marie, and Bernadette. Both families were part of the strong foundation of the Catholic community of St Mary's and active members of the Radcliffe family, especially after the war.

Anne Sweeney was from a large family of Kiernan's and one of the family cousins was Kitty Kiernan, the fiancé of the patriot Michael Collins. The family farm near Longford was then owned by her brother who in turn had a large family for future ownership, including Vincent, James, Brian Paddy, Barney, and Mary.

The fortunes of the family were to change for the better when the CAP was introduced, and land prices improved enabling overdrafts to be cleared and new houses to be built by the family who all had building trade skills. During the war years Carmel paid frequent visits to her cousins and this has continued over the years.

Carmel had then these great skills in domestic science and especially sewing crafts which were to make a significant contribution to bringing up our future family. She was also active in all the town events such as the annual parade when all Churches would take part by designing fancy dress floats. Because we were three years different in age groups, we had never met at school, but she was in the same class as my brother David.

I met Carmel on my return North having left De Havilland when we had apparently a Lonny Donnegan experience at Church when she spotted a "blond head with thick neck" young man in front of her and we then started socializing in a group of friends and occasionally went out as a couple to local social events, including a Christmas Party organized by The General Engineering at the Grand Hotel in Manchester, where we were entertained by a young Mike Yarwood.

The group attended both Bolton and Bury Palais and singing pubs around both Bolton and Bury. In addition, we socialized further afield in Manchester most of the time, but on the odd night out to Cleveleys to the Blue Dolphin. Generally, this group of friends would meet in the Rayner's Bar, onto the Two Tubs pubs and then onto Bury Palais before a visit to the 103 club for a night cap. Bolton was mainly for a tour of the singing pubs on Sunday night, the Toby Inn, the Black Dog, and the Wilton Arms in particular. Alan Jackson married Anne Shay in 1967, the first of the Rayner's friends to do so.

Manchester at that time was full of great night clubs and in particular, Tiffany's, Mr. Smith's, Dino's, and the Bossa Nova. The best Jazz club in Manchester at that time was the MSGwhere all the famous bands played on a regular basis. Bill Benny's club was a magnet for international stars and for the Chinese business owners who loved to gamble late into the night.

Our holidays at the General and Avanti became more ambitious and included trips to Spain on the Costas, to Majorca at C'an Pastilla and Jersey where we stayed at the Hotel De France and played friendly football matches against the Portuguese staff in 95 degrees F. We played golf on the noted La Moiré course, and once again experienced a beautiful Island and very friendly people. I met a family from Liverpool and became friendly with them and their daughter, who was to become my first girlfriend, and continued to visit them in Liverpool at weekends when at Avanti. For some reason, the friendship did not last, and I cannot remember why.

At Bolton we were entertained by Peter Lee orchestra and Alan Haven and his dynamic trio, which was to become famous in modern jazz circles. Bury Palais was more frenetic than Bolton and provided a mixture of bands to suit the wilder tastes of the Bury crowd.

The Rayner's remained our main watering hole and several of the customers would agree to make group visits with the owners, Bram, and Sheila Fisher. Bram was a trombonist with the BBC Northern Orchestra, and they had excellent contacts around the country which facilitated our trips to London, mixing with the musicians of the day at various clubs.

We made one short holiday trip to Germany visiting a music festival in Neuse near Dusseldorf and a boat trip down the Moselle Valley sampling the various wines, many which were not available in England. In Neuse, the festival included large selections of beer from all over Germany and full military style marching bands from around Europe and including the military bands of the British Army serving in the country.

The parade started at 8am for three days and before marching through the town all musicians were provided with a small very strong beer. All bands were judged on their outfits and their playing during a long day and several more beers. The pristine morning bands returned in the late afternoon a little worse for wear, out of step and out of tune, however they appeared for the second and third days in their pristine outfits.

What a fabulous experience of German lifestyles.

Our love of the Lake District started when we were invited by Alan Jackson to travel with the Venture Scouts of Rochdale for a week's camping, walking and climbing holiday to Borrowdale and the Langdale Pikes over the Easter period, and before I left for Africa we all drove up on Friday evening after work and arrived to erect the tent, which we achieved with help from the scouts, and then retired to the local Jennings pub for beers and songs, in the scouting tradition. The rains commenced just as we returned to our tents and within twenty minutes we were flooded, so much so that we had to seek refuge in the pub for an all-night lock-in and further songs, not in the scouting tradition. We had a great time, but this experience ended our camping forever. We continued to visit the District evert Easter, from wherever we were working, but always in either Hotel or Log Cabins, including the Old Dungeon Gyll Hotel and the New Dungeon Gyll Hotel, with our children. From climbing the Middle Fell Buttress to walking up Stikle Tarn was a clear indication that age was having an impact on our ambitions.

Carmel was a unique person and together we had a blessed married life of almost 51 years.

We met in the 1960's after I had returned North from Hatfield after the cancellation of the Top-Secret Blue Street Missile System which sent us on a different career path to an international life, and married in 1970 at St Mary's, by Fr John Curran.

As an only child Carmel quickly became the communicator for our large family keeping everyone in touch when we travelled overseas.

We lived and worked with 70 nationalities, and it was always Carmel who quickly established local contacts in her gregarious way.

They will always remember Carmel and not Bernard. Wherever we went Carmel gave support to all in need

We established our first home in Cunliffe Drive Sale Cheshire and rented accommodation in Seal Sands whilst working on the Ekofisk North Sea oil project.

On completion of this contract, and in order to be near Heathrow Airport for international commuting to Dubai, we bought our second family home in Hartley Wintney and stayed there for 32 years.

From Dubai we went first to Jubail in Saudi Arabia then to Jeddah and Riyadh

In 2004 both Michelle and Robert were married and in 2006 Carmel decided that after supporting me in my career and travelling wherever this took me, she wanted to "Return to the Hills in the North".

This we did in 2007 and we were the first to buy on the new Millbeck Lane development in 2008, where we have lived ever since.

My career took us around the world and included 14 mega engineering and construction projects and then 25 years in the Management Consultancy Business, a truly extra-ordinary international life and journey.

Carmel was extremely proud of the way that our three children had progressed in their chosen careers in life and in our gift of five grandchildren. She was looking forward to the birth of our sixth grandchild, Poppy Willow, on the third of June.

She had a great skill at making clothing, mastered the complicated macrame art and in later life completing crocheted blankets for each grandchild.

After spending the first 18 years of married life bringing up our family Carmel decided to assist at School and quickly found that she had a natural talent and understanding of dyslexia and commenced a one-to- one teaching career in special needs

Once again, she was instrumental in establishing the local community in Millbeck.

Carmel had a deep faith with a strong ethical approach to life in an increasingly self-serving and selfish world. She recently obtained an Irish passport, objecting strongly to a government that failed to address the needs of the people.

I was fortunate to be able to write our autobiography of our exciting life whilst on dialysis and with the help of Michelle publish the book in 2020. Carmel plays a major role throughout the book and records our journey in life and gives a clear picture of her full contribution. Carmel is in star position in a photo with Bobby Moore when the 1966 England team visited Dubai with the Queen to open the Dry Dock.

Some of my best photos were taken during this period, especially the birth of James.

For our 50th Wedding anniversary I was able to provide the content photos which James had converted into a life collection shown in the collage.

The pleasure Carmel has had from our grandchildren cannot be calculated and she will remain in their memories for the rest of their lives.

The shock we all have to come to terms with at Carmel's passing is a measure as to how loved she was by all who had the fortune to meet her in life. Please remember her in your prayers

Thank you all for attending this Requiem Mass today, at the Crematorium after and the reception arranged at St Joseph's Comm unity Hall after in order that we can help to celebrate such a fantastic life and help each other grief in private.

POEMS AND LYRICS

1.0	When the Virus Struck	Criminal Actions	
2.0	Ode to Carmel	Anniversary	14,02,2022
3.0	Lockdown	Loneliness	
4.0	Ode to George Floyd	Fight for life	
5.0	The Viral Pimpernel	Holding Government to account.	
6.0	For welfare of my child	Dominic Cummings	
7.0	Ode to Radcliffe	Decimated Town	
8.0	Radcliffe on Irwell	Ancient History	
9.0	It is your Moral Duty	Immoral PM feeling contrite.	
10.0	Leadership Lost	Lead by absence.	
11.0	The year Democracy Died	1974 removal by Tories of local representation.	
12.0	Party of Law-and-Order	Government Dogma	
13.0	House of Cowards	The unelected House	
14.0	Elbow Gate. Brave Boris.	Transmission. Of Virus	
15.0	If we never meet again.		
16.0	Fun was fun when we were young	Memories of youth.	
17.0	Empty streets of London	Covid impact Lyrics	
18.0	Please don't leave me	Response to Please Release Me.	
19.0	Tears in my Heart	Love song for Carmel.	
20.0	When we were young.		
21.0	Love is in the cloud.	Remote love song	
22.0	Poetry in Shielding	Lyrics in Lockdown.	
23.0	If you have the gift of life	Philosophy	
24.0	Missing you. At Christmas.	The pain of loss.	
25.0	Lost	Martha Riley Nine years old.	

[POEM]

WHEN THE VIRUS STRUCK

When the virus struck, we were totally unprepared,

But we had been warned, for more than twenty years.

By our epidemiologists, giving expert advice.

To arrogant, deaf ears, but dismissed in a thrice.

By our self-engrossed Political Leaders

Engrossed and full of their selfish, self-importance.

No sense or awareness of the impending chaos

That could be caused by this intelligent,

Corona Virus

Silent, swift, and mutating quickly

Deadly for us all; the young, the old

And especially all our frail and sickly!

Our underfunded NHS and care services,

Brought into battle with nothing but their courage.

Failed by our Party Dogma Driven Politicians,

And short of protective PPE.

Our front-line forces nurses and doctors

Our cleaners, our carers, our drivers,

Our porters and our helpers!

No resilience to fight, stripped out by Austerity.

Sent to fight the foe all naked

By Politicians with no conscience, apology, or humility

Now sent out to put their lives at risk.

And fearing the outcome with great uncertainty!

Unmasked, un-gowned the naked warriors went.

To fulfil their duty and care for their patients

A silent prayer before the battle

But many prayers remained unanswered.

The carers quickly became the cared for

To pay the ultimate sacrifice,

Increasing risk by double shifting

To fill the gap of no resources

And give their lives for their fellow humans.

In fighting the foe and all their giving

Still fighting still for a decent living

No rises for our band of heroes

Priority will go to those who lead us.

From a government, ignorant,

Uncaring and self-serving!

Having to rely on Captain Tom and people giving.

The fifth Wealthiest Nation relying on Charity funding.

Wake up wake up you Politicians.

Embrace Humility. Lose your arrogance.

Focus on your prime responsibility.

"Ensure the delivery of an affordable Health and Care Service from Cradle to Grave" NHSCGG.

Your measure of success is a quality of life for all.

The Challenge for you with lack of knowledge of epidemiology or practical infection control solutions.

Formulate and implement a Strategy to enable the delivery of your prime responsibility that will guarantee the future

Balanced Economy without destroying the Planet and acceptable quality of life for all.

The Radcliffe Lad
Kelbrook. Lancashire
20.03.2020

2

[POEM]

ODE TO CARMEL
(The Sadly Missed Matriarch)

You can cut through the sound of silence.
Waiting for footsteps at the door
No greetings to welcome you home any more.
No banter or small talk
The depth of the missing yet unmeasured
The absence of your greeting kissing is fading.
The sound of silence, silence, and silence

Not to see you anymore
Bring the memories back which flow.
Like the fast-running river
Battling all the barriers
As to the open see it flows. Reaching its goal
And silence once more

The silence of the phone
Is an indicator that you are not home?
Communicator in chief
With friends and family
So sadly missed, they all complain.
Never to hear your voice again.

Garden empty
Missing tender care
Avoiding all the playful tactics
Shortcuts unaware
To be chosen to live at all.
And experience life to the full
From humble beginnings
And meeting at all
A miracle of chance,
Or pre-destination
Or chance or luck
We will never know.
One plus one at our first meeting
Two strong and opposite forces
The needed yin and yang fitting into one.
Me, lights on and you, lights off.
Me closed doors and you always open.

A common purpose with all choices made.
With knowledge such to guide us
Through such our blessed lives
Living in such beauty
Such partnership as ours
We lost our first love at full term and more.
I will never forget your tears.
As I walked through the door.
Our baby wrapped in towels.
Carried by the nurse.
Passing me in the corridor
No name, no christening

No burial, only the incinerator!

Michelle followed quickly.
And then our third child Robert
All three by Caesarean section
Born with great fortitude.
At personal health risk

We were advised that if we tried for more.
You would be at significant risk.
Miraculously you recovered after some years.
And in Dubai you delivered James our fourth child
Another Caesarean

We were noted for our domestic debate.
You held your own with a pragmatic view on life.
You had a sixth sense of how to trust people at first sight.
Your management of domestic issues outstanding
Your ability to travel with such a young family incredible.

With your natural ability to quickly make friends
Hartley Wintney became our UK base for 32 years.
Our assimilation was quick and full,
In all village activities
Church, Saving Church, Twinning Associations,
Parish Council. Pastoral Parish Council Club, Football Club,
Golf Club
Hartley Wintney U3A, Cricket Club

In addition, you commenced your career in Special Needs teaching.
Your legacy with all the children you taught on a one to one,
With live with them through life

You then decided that you wished to Return to the Hills of your birth.
We achieved this in 2007 and settled in Kelbrook,
Which you quickly made our retirement home?

In your absence today there is no discussion or debate
No opportunity to say sorry, all too late.
Creative ideas drying up without the yin/yang approach.
Leaving empty mind and empty cup

No pleasures from shared memories
To keep our spirits up
In shielding and in lockdown
No parties cheese or wine we had so looked forward to
To share our long dark days of winter
Or fill our empty cup.
We missed so much.

How fortunate we were.
To live at the head of the parade
To see the Earth in all its glory
How our parents through the war
Sacrificed so much with so much succour.
Givers all and not takers
Based on faith and true believers

Carmel and I were indeed our Ying and Yang
Two halves in making one.
Your calling came too soon my love.
Leaving us all so broken hearted
Taking you to your well-earned rest
Only the best
Thank so much.
Love
Bernard

PS
While Angels sleep
Our PM cheats.
At all and every moment
But he cannot hide or run away.
From the spotlight that he craves
With all the Covid Victims
Lying in their graves
RIP

Bernard Heys
14.02.2022

3

[POEM]
LOCKDOWN

"Lockdown loneliness kills the spirit of the soul, the body and the mind."

The Marginalised.

Look after the poor, the needy and blind.

Remember always to be kind.

Look after the frail the elderly and weak.

Give what you can give and do not seek,

To receive return in any way

You will get tour reward one day.

Do not forget that your sick neighbour.

Has spent their life in honest labour.

Give them help whenever you can.

Take the wind off those.

Who do not have the strength to resist?

The forces of nature, of life and of disease

So, given to those who are most in need.

And keep them safe from daily greed.

From those in power who sow the seeds of Despair.

The Radcliffe Lad
Kelbrook Lancashire
25.04.2020

4

ODE TO GEORGE FLOYD

(In Memory of George Floyd)

With every breath I breathe today,
My only wish is, to live another day.
To live my life in work, in prayer and play!
Brothers and sisters help me here.
I cannot breathe and death is near.
Who will help me from this pain?
I may not see my child again.
I hope my death will not be in vain.
That peace and friendship will remain.
That the force for good that will emerge
And colour, creed, and gender merge
From thousands of years and our vale of tears
The past has gone, the present is here.
Let the whole world act to mend this tear.

The Radcliffe Lad
Kelbrook Cashier
30.05.2020

[POEM]
THE VIRAL PIMPERNEL

Introduction:

Coughs and Sneezes Spread Diseases.
A Poem for the protection of Children
Please remember the Neotree Charity No 1186748 in your
prayers and in your giving.

Bernard Heys
The Radcliffe Lad
Kelbrook Lancashire
15.05.2020 19.30
bernieheys@gmail.com
07484246126

Early childhood memories.
Ring a Ring a Rosie
A pocket full of poise
Atishoo! Atishoo!
We all fall-down.

"The Viral Pimpernel":

Can't see him	Eyes
Can't hear him	Ears
Can't taste him	Tongue
Can't feel him	Fingers
Can't smell him	Nose

Beware the Viral Pimpernel

If we cannot see him, or hear him, or taste him, or feel him like all life we will have to find a way to smell him. (See my article on Olfactometers).

I have added this today to try and simplify and for children to learn and understand when returning to School:

Remember Schoolchildren:

THE VIRAL PIMPERNEL

If you want to cough or sneeze, put your head between your knees.
Cover mouth and nose with hand or hanky or your sleeve.
If you lose your taste or smell, tell your Mum or Dad, you feel unwell.
If your skin begins to blister, make sure that you tell your sister.
If your chest begins to ache tell the world for God's sake.
If you find it hard to breathe, ask for help immediately.
If you have a chill or fever, also seek a quick reliever.
If you feel a little confused do not move in your shoes.
So, keep yourself, your friends and family safe.
Make sure that you always cover your face.
Stay away from others and create your own space.
Self-check your temperature every day,

Before you go to work, school, or play.

Wash your hands, your arms and face.

So, keep your distance when you are playing.

And keep your distance when you are praying.

When you return to school, please stay safe and keep the rule.

Remember that enclosed spaces can spread infections.

And ventilation systems do not always give protection.

To repel the silent and swift new virus,

Which is very clever at avoiding detection?

Free external space is the best barrier.

Against this virulent-intelligent attacker!

Please take care and do not fear, always know that help is near.

6

FOR THE WELFARE OF MY CHILD

(Dominic Cummings)

For the welfare of my child

I woke him up at twelve.

Carefully placed him in my motor.

With myself and symptomatic mother

When are we going to get there?

I need a drink and a wee

Do not worry we will keep you safe.

All locked up in this very small space.

When we get there don't be sad

We'll keep you close to your mum and dad.

We are so sorry you became so sick on this trip.

But our great NHS did the trick.

And made you better.

Your test was negative thank God.

Not for me though I am invincible.

My eyes are dim I cannot see.

I'll take you and your mum for a test drive with me.

Sixty miles should do the trick.

To the Castle we will go

Arriving safely if I do not drive too quick.

Avoiding others on the way

Let's pray we live another day.

The Radcliffe Lad

Kelbrook Lancashire

31.05.2020

For the record: Submissions by the Author to the BBC

BBC Comments.	25.05.2020
CAS-6080756-G0Y852	24.05.2020
CAS-6082295-L3G126	24.05.2020
CAS-6083651-J7K5M7	25.05.2020
CAS-6083809-Z4V2TS	25.05.2020

7

[POEM]
ODE TO RADCLIFFE

Bernard Heys bernieheys@gmail.com 12.11.2018

My wife Carmel and I visited the town on 11.11.2018 and I could not but stop to reflect on the devastation inflicted on the town since incorporation into the Metropolitan Borough of Bury, and diversion of businesses and footfall from the Town and centre.

> What have they done to the town we knew so well?
> There were mines and mills for cotton and paper products.
> There were shuttle cocks, spindles, and rolls.
> There were shirts, dresses, and Macintoshes.
> There was dying, bleaching, and anodizing.
> There were valves and penstocks and sluice gates.
> There was heavy engineering of every discipline.
> There were high speed machines for cable production.
> There were extruders and payoffs and barrel packers.
> There were brewers and coopers and dray horses too.
> There were farms, allotments, and gardens.
> There was fishing, boating, and sailing too.
> There were bakers and grocers and onion makers.
> There were millers, turners, drillers, and borers.
> There was casting, welding, forming, and shaping.
> There was tin bashing and soldering and planning.
> There were carpenters and cabinet makers.
> There were pattern makers and machine setters.

There was brick making and house building.
There was sand and gravel for infrastructure projects.
There were Council Powers to control and manage.
There were Council Services to meet local needs.
There were communities working together for common purpose.
There was cricket, football, rounders, and tennis.
There were champion swimmers and snooker players.
There were cricket legends and Oscar Winners.
There were social clubs for all persuasions.
There were trams, trains, omnibuses, and charabancs.
There were schools, churches, and libraries too.
There were Whit Parades and festivals.
There were cinemas and swimming pool and Civic Halls.
There were Technical Colleges and Secondary schools.
There were brass and silver bands and concert parties too.
There were parks for walking, bowling, and boating.

Big Brother 1974 Off the cliff.
The year direct democracy died for all our communities.
"What have they done to the town we loved so well?"

May I suggest that the representatives of the rival groups visit the East Lancashire towns of Colne and Barnoldswick in order to see what can be achieved with adequate representation?

All the towns which had their subsidiarity rights removed in 1974 form a shared value group to challenge that decision in order to ensure a speedy return to direct local democracy.

Radcliffe Revival Group: The only way to change is from the bottom up and this group have embarked on a mammoth task of returning power to the local community by multiple projects and efforts to gain council representation and formulate a town strategy and is deserving of the full support of old and new Radcliffe residents.

The group failed through lack of support.

I became aware of Radcliffe First in February of 2020 and joined the group which had a similar purpose as expressed in my Autobiography.

Bernard Heys MCMI. CWIFM. DipBs.
Kelbrook
15.03.2019

8

[POEM]

RADCLIFFE ON IRWELL

Our first recorded residents
Arrived 6000 years ago.
Where they came from
Or where they went to
We really do not know.
They built their houses on the river.
Piling deep into the mud
With superstructures, all carved and
Made from wood.
A simple life to catch the fish.
To give them all
Their daily dish
The evidence was clear.
The residents had no deer.
Their cousins in Ireland
Had long been cut off.
By waters from the Ice age
And left them alone.
To continue with their foraging!
No evidence of stone construction,
No signs of the flood destruction.
Then came the Celts.
The first invasion
With their skills of cloth and gold

The Romans came with their great Empire.
With building skills and fearless warriors
To rule and educate with language.
To tame the ground with roads and bridges
And walls to contain the Northern tribes.
Of painted Picts and all their wives
The years they stayed they did not waver.
To integrate and take the favour!
Their energies all spent.
The visitors were homesick,
So, home they went!
The Danes were quick to fill the void.
Raiding from across the sea
On the Northeast of these Isles,
Quite regularly!
Not slow to follow from across the water.
Tribes galore for pillage and slaughter
The Saxons and the Angles
The Angles in the Anglia
The Saxons to Northumbria
And the Jutes in Yorkshire
Small kingdoms they made wherever they stayed.
But no evidence to Radcliffe they made.
William arrived in 1066,
And kicked the Saxons from Sussex and Essex!
Who took to their boats in great fear!
And sailing far across the seas
They made their homes.
In the land of Crimea!
The Saxons of Northumbria,

Were made of stronger stuff.

They held their ground and Castles too.

And allowed their daughters to marry the Normans.

Including the sons of Roger De Poitou!

The De Radcliffe's came, our land to claim.

And thus, the name of Radcliffe came.

But better than that and to our surprise

In searching for my Station in Life

Our great ancestral path we traced,

From Ireland, from Scotland, from Wales,

From Northern Scandinavian and Northern France

And the ancient Royal Family of Ogle

The Saxons of Northumbria!

And the Royal House of the Earls of Errol

The Hay Clan of Fife,

What a life to tell our children

Who would a thought it, Radcliffe Lad?

Certainly not your dad or grandad

We so called English always willing to fix.

Now find us.

Are truly a mongrel mix.

The Radcliffe Lad

Kelbrook Lancashire

10.06.2020

9

IT IS YOUR MORAL DUTY

It is your moral duty.

The PM said.

Listen to me,

And you will finish up dead.

At birth, my father named me fair.

After great leaders of history

To prepare me for

The highest ministry!

At school we were taught

The rule how to rule.

The people of this Country

No skills no knowledge, just a bluffer

Become a fool, a clubber and duffer.

Preparing for my first position

In writing sleazy journalism

On the working class of Marxism

Their lack of morals and reliability

Attracted me to show them.

That I could do better.

I joined them in their base activity.

I sewed my seed, left right and centre.

Politics were not my ambition.

So, I made no differentiation.

I chose my several wives.

With selective discretion
To my surprise my fortunes prospered
Despite my youthful games, and indiscretions
My party thinking that my bluster.
Would be the best Mayor of London
They could muster.
Mayor of London and public person
Fooled the lot and got promotion.
Quietly plotting for the future
Not satisfied with minor positions
Not supporting the incumbent ministers
Undermining at every opportunity
Austerity I supported for ten long years.
When the rich got richer,
And the poor get poorer.
Keep him quiet and give him.
Foreign Secretary for his sins
Little Englander lost overseas.
His first assignment went foul and rotten.
With poor Nazim, in jail forgotten!
Along the way he found Rasputin
Ex-aide to his best friend
His Brutus garden gnome
Not a fit person to be PM,
Declared the sad gnome!
I told the wife my Lady Macgnome
E. Tu my friend dear Michael Gove.
Rasputin then released by Michael,
Becomes the Dom, advice to recycle.
A latter-day Rasputin stating that.

Brexit was a dumb idea.
To re-unite the Tory Party!
But hearing him wrong,
The ambitious would-be new leader
He took his advice and,
Used the 'Brexit' as his power Mantra!
Launched his bid for power with banter!
Taking back control of
My kingdom of Little England
Previously held by
Matt Lucas and David Walliams.
So, do as I say and not as I do.
Your Moral Duty for your Country
No morals required for your gentry.

The Radcliffe Lad.
Kelbrook Lancashire
16.08.2020

10

[POEM]
LEADERSHIP LOST

The carrion call for leadership came.

Headless and chicken the name of the game

I lead from the front by

Whipping the pack

To succeed in the hunt and never look back.

No mind of their own, no choice but to say yes.

Failure to follow, results in the sack.

Learn to cluck and pluck,

And muck things up.

Remember tomorrow my friends.

You fail and I will elevate you to the Lords.

It is all that awaits you at the end,

Reward for failure is the name of the game.

So, weaving and ducking your way through the mire

Will give you rewards to meet your desire.

Take back control and follow the pack.

Forward, upward sideways, and back

Do not worry, do not stress.

Follow your leader, the failed Eton Mess

The working class that I once vilified.

Believed what I said.

They voted me in because.

They were petrified.

To Level up was my first sworn word

So, I ennobled my 36 friends,

To the very well paid the House of Lords.

To take the cheap wine and easy money

The privileges and perks with the other jerks.

What about all the key workers you praised so well?

Key workers all, thanks for my life, I praise.

But sorry to say you will not get a raise.

We have been guided by the scientific advice.

But we know better and made our indecision.

Before thinking twice

Stay at home and risk infection,

Within closed spaces and no large garden

The case for face masks is weak,

From ignorance or political persuasion?

Said the Chief Medical Officer

And will not give you any protection.

Save the NHS they said and say your prayers,

Because we have underfunded for the past ten years

We set up Public Health England

With staff the best in the World But fired them all,

To compensate for all our failures!

And cover the backs of our Ministerial Quacks.

Obvious their lining up the scientists

For blame at the future inquest

We are lacking in objective evidence.

The headless chicken can only go so far.

Before we are all fully,

Exposed to the blame game!
We need Government accountability now.
Where have all the yes men gone?
Seeking favours, everyone!

The Radcliffe Lad
Kelbrook Lancashire
06.08.2020

11

[POEM]

THE YEAR DEMOCRACY AND COMMUNITIES DIED

1974

In 1974 we were told that our subsidiarity
Foundation of our vaunted democracy
And not yet one hundred years old
Would be sacrificed, to our ruling autocracy.
Removed without ceremony or clarity of purpose.
The God of Central Government
With local powers removed from people of
Integrity, intelligence, honesty, and authority
A central power base of ignorant mediocrity
Stripped of their basic legal human rights
No Council, no Mayor, no Aldermen no representation.
Communities destroyed for following generations.
Direct services removed and facilities decaying.
The soul ripped out and children crying.
The backbone of the Country
Ripped apart for Party Dogma!
Wake up, wake up you headless chickens.
Before we return to the days of Dickens
The rule of subsidiarity must be returned to
Give the people and communities some clarity.
And some certainty that they will elect a team.

Who understand their dreams and needs?

Built on the sweat and tears of their ancestral deeds.

Speaking with the same broad accent

A team who understands their commitment,

To the call for help in any predicament!

The need to turn the clock back.

Before the year of 1974!

The Radcliffe Lad
Kelbrook Lancashire
24.08.2020

12

THE PARTY OF LAW AND ORDER

We are the party of Law and Order
But we are far better at jaw, jaw.
We make the rules for you to follow.
With promises, so weak and hollow
Nothing that we say and do.
Is pure publicity for you?
To vote us in as honest brokers
More fool you, you poor blind suckers.
To believe us chicken Tory Plücker's
Our vision for a fairer future
For fairer taxes, fairer sharing
Fairer health and fairer caring
We will defend your right to democracy.
So, we shackle all our MP's.
With our Autocracy
To follow me like sheep to slaughter
Yes, men to the last with weary, tired.
Sloping shoulders
No mind or conscience of their own
They are only there to support my throne.
To be elected for our failures
To uphold the Law
For which our Dogma stands for
Not for us the petty thieving,

We jail all those.

With families grieving!

Do not do as we do.

But make sure you do as we say.

And listen very carefully.

We uphold the values of trust, of honesty.

Of integrity, of respect for the law and authority

For we are honourable men

But like all men are weak

And in the end posterity we seek

To gain our place in history!

The Radcliffe Lad
Kelbrook Lancashire
14.09.2020
"Authors Prediction in his Autobiography":

13

[POEM]

THE HOUSE OF COWARDS

Where have all the strong men gone?

Turned into cowards everyone!

Yes, we will we say as one.

Yes, we will all comply,

Becomes their only, stock reply!

We will follow our pied piper.

Heading off to meet the cliff,

With our scruffy blond fat blighter!

We are after all the party of law and order.

But blindly led happily to the slaughter!

Our values and beliefs are based on medieval Aristocracy.

Which by the way has nothing to do with direct Democracy?

Or come to that Subsidiarity.

We are all born equal,

With equal opportunity

But we know better,

An act with impunity1

We negotiate with skill and flair.

With leader on white horse,

And flaxen hair!

If only we could understand agreements,

To save us from our future appeasements

It only took us three long years.

With process failures ending in tears!

Never mind our word is our bond.
We are men of honour and true.
If you don't believe us, then feck to you
We have only one clear objective,
To get Brexit done and exit
To take back control with the oven ready pie
As we stated in our Manifesto forty times
Regrets that the pie was undercooked.
Perhaps we made the pastry too hasty.
Too many cooks with no experience
Were sent to Brussels with empty portfolio.
To put our Country first
Blinded by Double and Triple Trappist,
To quench our thirst!
Behind our mask a cunning plan
Was my own insatiable for power?
After all I had ambitions to follow my hero
Who sadly failed and finished zero?
After all it is all Greek to me,
Or was I Turkish, or even German!
The only skills we need in Government.
Pick those who will sign a covenant.
If they fail, you can always elevate.
To the House of seasoned yes men
To meet their foes and all can celebrate.
My Manifesto will reform this house of sin.
By letting thirty-six of my friends in
Just as well incompetence pays.
So, we can continue in our privileged ways.
We will therefore change the Law at will.

Take back Control and get Brexit done.
Lose all our friends, our trade and credibility.
We will promise all and try our best.
To redress the failures of myself and predecessors
We may however finish like the Marie Celeste,
In protecting our democracy.

The Radcliffe Lad
Kelbrook Lancashire
16.09.2020

14

[POEM]
BORIS THE EDUCATED
(Postscript 14.04.2021)

The theatrical actions of the PM in his ostentatious greeting by bare knuckle to bare knuckle and bare elbow to bare elbow has created a fashion using the second most virulent transmission path and breaking the social distance rules.

This Government have failed to implement the recommendations of the two major Pandemic Preparedness Reports discussed in my book "The Stealthy Viral Pimpernel." They have accordingly had to spend billions on emergency supplies that would not have been a requirement had they been prepared as advised in the reports. A complete dereliction of duty.

The pied piper of the Tory party pulling all those who signed up to his instruction to conform or die heading for the cliff and extinction. As per my prediction beware the big bad wolf has struck with a vengeance with his Svengali Rasputin companion. The Dark Clouds have become darker, and our future looks increasingly grim.

If allowed to continue he will isolate the Country from all our friends.

Rumours are that he does not attend or lead the critical Cobra meetings but does his usual disappearing act.

His historic dismissal of the working class as evidenced in his so-called journalistic career and articles written purely to draw attention to himself.

Communities have been stripped of their soul by Central Government removing their Subsidiarity Rights to self- govern but at the same time removing funding to leave the whole Country without any resilience to face the future.

The theatrical actions of the PM in his ostentatious greeting by bare knuckle to bare knuckle and bare elbow to bare elbow has created a fashion using the second most virulent transmission path and breaking the social distance rules.

To record this, I have written an additional postscript poem to add to the Anthology.

Bare knuckle to bare knuckle
Bare elbow to bare elbow
Transmit the virus at will.
The bold brave Boris
In his Shakespearean thrill
Showboating again his ego
For all the people to see
To show the people how brave he is
How much knowledge he possesses?
To challenge the virus
And grab it by the throat.
Be to the immune Buccaneer.
With less than a little between the ears.
My expert knowledge of viral transmission

Saved by the brave front liners.
Why saved my life and viral remission.
How foolish how ignorant
Is it possible to be, except with him?
Beware all those who follow.
In the steps of this fool, so hollow
Who acts the Court Jester, the Clown?
Who atishoo, atishoo?
We will all fall down.
Into the hollow
Made for them in the ground.
Boris the brave
Without fear he will go
Bare knuckle to bare knuckle
Bare elbow to bare elbow
Leaving behind those he touched
Contemplating, a trip to the grave.

15

IF WE NEVER MEET AGAIN

If we never meet again
We had fun along the way.
Our time filled with love.
With care and consideration
For each other's dreams
And a fulfilled life in future
No, me No you only but only two.
If we never meet again
We had fun along the way.
Together, forward, no constraints
Winning, Losing, no complaints
Will things last, we do not know?
In spring, in summer, in autumn and the snow
Learning, listening forward we would go.
Creating, failing, and achieving
Together forward no constraints
The past is past the future looming.
With path ahead unknown
With many stations on the road
And meeting many cross-roads

With joys and sorrows, around the corner
Friends forever and
Together forward no complaints.

The Radcliffe Lad
Kelbrook Lancashire
21.09.2020

16

FUN WAS FUN WHEN WE WERE YOUNG

Gone are the days when we were young.
Carefree, careless, climbing, falling,
Bruised and battered, nothing mattered.
When we were young.
Those carefree days are gone forever.
No longer free to roam at will.
To fish the Dingle for perch or gudgeon
Tree swinging and brid neezing.
Fun was fun when we were young.
On the farm we learned our skills
The smell of hay, as we drove the dray.
The chicken free to roam.
Not all cooped-up, like most today.
Feed the pigs and geese and milker's, every day.
Fun was fun when we were young.
Rally-voe we played all night.
Chasing shadows dark and scary.
In tip latch games we took a risk
If caught or worse subject to a snitch
Far better to stick to marbles or murps,
With lead or glass eyes on a different pitch.
Fun was fun when we were young.
Peggy up and Peggy down a real game of skill
Demanding hand and eye co-ordination

To make the final kill.
Roller skating fast and furious.
Ignoring all especially the curious
Round and round the avenues
Of the new estate and into town.
Fun was fun when we were young.
Jobs galore we did for sixpence.
Fixed rate earnings for our efforts
Running errands for old ladies,
Chopping firewood for fire kindling
Delivering each Saturday morning
Bright and early before the dawning.
Second shift of the day rag and bone collected.
Fun was fun when we were young.
Growing up we moved our skills up.
Milk deliveries with Shire horses
And floats that would grace Cinderella.
Making bricks at Crowther's yard
Collecting pig swill from posh houses.
Fun was fun when we were young.
To Thornleigh College we did go
But in the summer to the mills
Lancashire Cotton Felt to give us thrills.
And to relieve the dirt and grime.
A prized appointment, with the Town parks department
Clean fresh air and nature free.
Fun was fun when we were young.
The bobby on the bear always on our street
Smart, erect well dressed and neat.
Solid walk and eyes like an eagle

Missed nothing at all.
Watching, supporting, guiding, and chastising
Vigilant through day and night
Making sure we were safe and all right.
Fun was fun when we were young.
We got in trouble once or twice.
And finished up before the magistrate.
The fear of God before and after,
The serious faces old and creased.
Strict and fair but with no laughter.
Let us off with strict admonition.
Father angry at our precarious position.
Fun was not fun when we were older.

The Radcliffe Lad
Kelbrook Lancashire
21.09.2020

17

[LYRICS]

EMPTY STREETS OF LONDON

Sing to Ralph McTell Streets of London
Have you seen the lone man?
As he jogs the streets of London
Weaving his way from his fellow man
He picks his steps with care.
To say hello or morning there
In case he breaks the law.
He knows he may be timed out.
By the local bobby on the beat
If he moves within two metres
Whilst walking on the street
So how can you tell me?
That you do not fear the virus
Of the killer coming near
You're first outside adventure.
Completed without fear.
Wash your hands, your face, and your eyes.
Wear your mask, your gown, your gloves,
Keep your distance do not sneeze.
Please keep calm and do not freeze.

The Radcliffe Lad
Kelbrook Lancashire.
24.03.2020

18

[LYRICS]

PLEASE DON'T LEAVE ME

B. Heys March 2015. (Music: Please Release Music.)
One of the songs I performed at my 70th birthday party was "Please Release Me"
which went down very well with our guests. I was quietly pleased. However, when we arrived home my wife admonished me with a thump in the back because she felt that I had delivered the song as if it were a personal insult to her and so the song was removed from my repertoire. I could then not repeat the performance at my 75th birthday party but believe that the tune deserves to be aired in a more positive context and therefore have penned the lyrics below, which reflect the reverse message of the original sentiments.

Please don't leave me, do not go.
For I still love you more and more.
To leave me now would be the end,
Believe in me, and the love I send.
To let our true love in and stay with me my friend.
We have always been so nearby,
Our love was (so) strong and without fear.
To leave me now would break my heart.
And Tear my body and soul apart.
Believe me now and let full love in.
Please don't leave me, do not go.
For I still love you more and more.

If we can start our life again

Our love will last until the end.

To leave me now would be a sin.

So, believe me and let our full love win.

(The original song is from 1946-49 by Eddie Miller, Robert Young and James Petworth. Made famous by Englebert Humperdinck in 1967. BMI 124 1220)

19

TEARS IN MT HEART

(Love song for Carmel [10.11.2919 - 20.02.2023])

*Timings are estimated and arranged to fit the melody, **Bernard**.*

Intro 40 secs

There were tears in my heart,
When you said you were leaving?
There were signs in my soul.
When you said you would go?

3 secs

After all we have been through
From the first time we met
We have fought all our battles.
With no fear or regret

3 secs

We have made up and made love.
Whenever we fought
Had four beautiful children.
A gift from above.

3secs

We lost our first child.
At the time of his birth
Which left us both grieving?
No time on this earth
No chance to name him.
Or a warm place to lay.
Remembered in our prayers.
With love every day

3 secs

We travelled the whole world.
No time to reflect.
On the beauty we saw there
And the lasting effects

3 secs

Admired the genius before us.
Creations and art
Of those great ancient people
Before they depart

3 secs

There are still tears in my heart.
So please change your mind
To find our Valhalla
Leaving trouble behind

3 secs

Life's journey continues.
In this sad vale of sorrow

But the sun and the moon
Will be shining tomorrow.

3 secs

We give thanks for a great life.
And the future to come.
Wipe the tears from my heart now.
Welcome home, welcome home.

3 secs

There are smiles in my heart now.
You have decided to stay.
My love forever
What more can I say

25 secs

20

WHEN WE WERE YOUNG

We met when we were young.
And stayed together always.
Through sun, wind, and rain
Our love remained the same.
Remember when,
We first went out together.
The Fields of grass were green.
And the blowing corn was yellow.
The chickens then roamed free.
And the pigs were full and fallow.
The time went fast.
When we were young
As fast as the swooping swallow
Then came the war one morning.
Like a blackbird without warning
We had to part,
No time to say goodbye.
My training started,
For jumping from the sky
In foreign lands with memories sustaining
Surviving on my military training
The time that passed did not destroy us.
Returning safe, well, and joyous
Before too long our numbers increased

One, two, three, four before we ceased.
Our fortunes hard to come by
In times of post war rationing
Re-building lives did not come easy.
But strength of faith and family values
With grandparents, Uncles and Aunties
Propping up our daily needs
No longer young but full of vigour
We made our mark and left our legacy.
To our children,
And our grandchildren
For their future and prosperity!

The Radcliffe Lad
Kelbrook Lancashire
16.08.2020

21

LOVE IS IN THE CLOUD

Love is in the cloud.
When you are around
The shimmer of the skies
Are reflected in your eyes.
Shadows beaming to the ground.
And love is on the wing.
With birds in flight far up above
Swooping, swaying on songs of love.
Time is eternal but we are not.
Life is for living and we are here today.
No time to lose but not to delay.
Love is in the cloud with souls for companions.
Riding the Cosmos in time regulation
Back to their home to find their salvation.
Never meeting those who started their journey, before them
Until the final, final reckoning
Reward for living, giving, and loving.

The Radcliffe Lad
Kelbrook Lancashire
21.09.2020

22

POETRY IN SHIELDING
LYRICS IN LOCKDOWN

(To poetry in motion) (10 min 10.10.2020)

Poetry in shielding

With you by my side

Poetry in shielding

With no place to hide

Poetry in shielding

No going out today

Poetry in lockdown

Down and down and down

Poetry in lockdown

Same thing day by day

Poetry in lockdown

We never go out and play.

Poetry in lockdown

Stay at home I say.

Poetry in lockdown

No meeting with the family

Poetry in lockdown

Avoid your neighbours too.

Poetry in lockdown

We like to make you blue.

Poetry in shielding

From the virus and the flu

Poetry in shielding

High risk older people

Sorry but you are back of the queue.

And locked away together.

Lonely, isolated, left alone to stew.

Poetry in shielding

Tomorrow is today.

Poetry in shielding

Forget your fun and play.

Poetry in shielding

Better stay home and pray.

Poetry in lockdown

Deeper and deeper in debt

Poetry in Lockdown

With the inquest yet to come

Government protesting still.

That since the start

They have done all they can.

Stubborn and unyielding,

The truth has yet to come.

Poetry in failing.

Grenfell as the marker

Blame the emergency services.

Not the root cause of the problem

Government apathy and lack of action planning

I accept full responsibility, the PM said.

After all I can lie to Parliament, and not be censured.

Poetry in shielding

When will we see the sun?

Our loved ones and our friends?
Will this go on forever?
Who do we turn to next?
Now with compulsory masks
And next the gloves if we are wise.
With a total lack of knowledge and great incompetence
Of listening to our scientists and their clear advice
Of consulting with Engineers experienced in applying
The science to practical prevention programmes for
Infection control and Saving Lives

In Memory of all those who have died and been affected by the sheer incompetence and criminal negligence before, during and after the Pandemic.

The Radcliffe Lad
Kelbrook Lancashire
10.10.2020

23

IF YOU HAVE THE GIFT OF LIFE

If you have the gift of life
Give thanks each day before the night.
Use your talents for the many
Give to receive as St Francis said.
So, say your prayers before you go to bed.
Seek not reward but put smiles on faces.
Of those in need and marginalised
Keep them safe, healthy, and well fed.

Count your blessings every day.
In sleeping, waking, work, rest, and play
Love your neighbour as yourself.
Honour your mother and your father
Love your brothers, sisters too.
Welcome dawn with open arms.
Open mind to worldly charms
Nurture Nature our great provider
Light and life from every seed
Colours of spring and every bulb
Born from simple slime and mould.

As the dawn approaches
And energy is spent.
We thank our God, for blessings sent.

The Radcliffe Lad
Kelbrook. Lancashire
20.04.2020

24

MISSING YOU AT CHRISTMAS

(Bernar Heys)

MISSING YOU AT CHRISTMAS
WE MISS YOU IN THE MORNING
WE MISS YOU THROUGH THE DAY
BUT MOST OF ALL
WE MISS YOU IN THE NIGHT
THE LONELY WALLS TO FACE
WITHOUT YOUR WARM EMBRACE

CHRISTMAS TIME WAS SPECIAL FOR YOU
AS AN ONLY CHILD
SEEKING FRIENDS AT HOLIDAY TIME
SINGING YOUR FAVOURATE CAROLS
MULLED WINE AND WHISKEY TOO

THE GARDEN MISSES YOU
YOUR LOVING TENDER CARE
PREPARING ALL THE FLOWERS, AND PLANTS
WITH YOUR FAMILY ARRIVING TO SHARE

THE WINTER MONTHS WITH FAMILY
WITHOUT YOUR PRESENCE HERE
THE SHARING OF MEALS AND DRINKS
THE CARDS THE TREE AND MISTLETOE

YOUR SOLID FAITH AND JOY OF LIFE
YOUR SKILLS IN TEACHING SPECIAL NEEDS
TO CHILDREN EVERYWHERE
YOUR FRIENDSHIPS MADE
AROUND THE WORLD
YOUR LOYALTY TO ALL YOU MET

THAT FATEFUL DAY I WILL NEVER FORGET

25

LOST MARTHA

INTRODUCING MARTHA RILEY, 9 YEAS OLD, WITH HER BEAUTIFUL AND HAUNTING POEM "LOST"

MARTHA RILEY
Published in: "Poetry in Shielding, Lyrics in Lockdown"

Inspiration:

The way I came up with this poem is I was feeling sad, but I wrote the poem instead. I got happier because I was writing my thoughts through poems, but I accelerated my emotions to make it sound better. I got happier as I wrote it so that's how it went from depressing to accelerating. Martha Riley

1.0

Lost in a cold-hearted world.
With no one around me
Never wanted to show my face.
Cos I'm lost in a cloud of darkness.

2.0

Blinded by the hatred and nightmare.
And I'm a magnet to despair.
Halloween coming every day.
Tricks but no treating.

3.0

Cos I'm lost, lost, lost.
In the never-ending despair
Ooh, I'm lost, lost, lost.

4.0

Trudging across the never-ending wasteland
Trying to get back to myself.
To get back home and to my bed
Trying to reach the people I love.

5.0

Warmth grappling towards me.
Cutting a path in the endless abyss
Climbing my way up to the light
Pulling my limbs like never
Now I'm found.

6.0

Free from the never-ending cell.
Free to roam the World as I like.
Coming back to the hugs of my family
Just like being born anew.

7.0

Unclouding my glasses,
Seeing the world in its glory,
Welcomed again by the human race.
Letting smiles and laughter, fill my heart.

8.0

The silhouette of happiness running towards me
Detailed lines in my eyes
Feeling warmth like never
Starting my life again.

ADDENDUM A

My journey to Writing and Publishing
First Person book writing experience
21.08.2020

My planned life-long career in the Aerospace Industry was suddenly halted after six years by our Government deciding to cancel our major leading-edge Blue Streak Missile Programme. This effectively put us out of the space race as a major player.

This prompted a change in direction of my career and set me on a completely different path and spectacular journey to achieve prominence in the International Engineering and Construction of fourteen mega projects around the world over a period of thirty-one years, working and living with seventy nationalities.

It also meant that I return North for my employment and met my wife and the most incredible international career and proud of three highly successful children and grandchildren, proving that there is a purpose in everything.

I then established my own Company and for the next twenty-five years delivering Management, Technical and Consultancy Services to Government bodies and Blue-Chip Companies around the Globe.

Several times during my life friends had suggested that I write my life story to record the unusual path I had taken starting as an apprentice with no University education.

After reaching seventy-two years of age, I had to retire through ill health and commenced to outline the purpose and content of my life story. The first purpose was to highlight the removal of the democratic process from my hometown and lack of recognition of my Church and community from any book on the town.

In 2015 however I became seriously ill and spent the next two years on home dialysis, nine hours each night for seven days per week and if the machine malfunctioned, I had to phone America for help in the middle of the night.

The response from America was "please can you tell us the serial number of the machine."

Being hooked up the machine and nine fluid bags was very restricting, I then transferred to haemodialysis for three days per week and four hours each therapy; this allowed me to complete my book by my 80th birthday on 10.11.2019.

My Consultant Daughter Dr Michelle Heys then completed the final proof reading, formatting, and Editing and after carrying out due diligence on several printers we visited Book Empire in Leeds to verify the production options and processes and to ensure that our files were compatible with their needs.

We appointed them and submitted our document with separate cover on 10.12.2019 and the first Edition was published locally on 12.01.2020.

Again, after due diligence checks we appointed New Generation to convert the Hard Copy version into the Amazon Kindle version.

ADDENDUM B

Writing on dialysis.

After immediately I had submitted my Autobiography to the printer on 10.12.2019 I decided to write an article for both NKF Dialysis and Diabetes UK with the purpose of thanking the teams of medics, nurses and support staff who had been looking after my serious conditions for the past four years, had brought me back to reasonable health and enabled me to both write and publish my book over 4,500-man hours during my dialysis therapy in Skipton Renal Unit.

I submitted the article to both organisations and waited.

Neither acknowledged the submission, which seems to be the fashion these days, so in January I sent a chaser email and NKF responded and suggested that I add to the article to comment on my experiences of dialysis during the lockdown.

I was delighted that the combined article was accepted for publication and appeared in the summer issue of the NKF Magazine.

I have continued to write to the powers that be in order to push for Diabetes to be recognised as a life changing illness and to be included in the NHS ten-year plan issued in 2019.

I wrote to the Chief Medical Officer, but again with no response. I sponsored a petition on Change.org to get testing done before therapy. I hope the reader will support any national petition when launched in late 2020, in support of the Renal Community.

The article is included below in order to familiarise the reader with some of the issues the community face, especially in times of the pandemic.

Kidney Care UK Dialysis:

Before I start my Article, I wish to thank all the Staff at the following: Airedale and St Luke's Cardiac Team: Airedale Diabetes Team: Bradford BRI. Renal Unit: Bradford St Luke's Renal Team: Skipton Renal Unit Team and Interserve Home Nurses.

Their amazing skill and care have enabled me to complete my Autobiography and follow up with this Article which I hope will give hope to all suffering from this debilitating illness.

After a 32-year career in Mega Engineering and Construction Projects around the World I decided to form my own Company giving advice based on my experience. Two months later I was diagnosed with Type 2 Diabetes at the age of 48. Starting with diet then medication and then to Insulin Control over the next 30 years. At age 72 my kidneys started to fail, and my diet had to change again to deal with this problem and I was placed on Insulin. At age 75 my kidneys totally failed whilst on holiday in Fuengirola and returning home I was given the choice of dialysis. Kidney Transplant was not an option. I initially chose PD Home Dialysis and spent two years at home on a bedside machine for 9 hours each night for 7 days per week. If the machine failed in the night, I had to phone America for help, usually having to terminate the therapy. My weight ballooned to 105 kg with fluid retention, and I had a massive heart attack. I was in ICU for two weeks and my weight reduced by 25kg through constant dialysis. I was then fitted with a stent. For twelve months everything went well before I started to feel chest pains again and in Nov 2018, I was re-admitted with a second less severe heart attack. On the operating table I overheard the Surgeon, nurses and Consultant discussing the situation which turned out to be the collapse of the Stent. There words were very disturbing "we do not like using these cheap stents." I commented that I hope they fit a better more reliable version!

We then agreed with the Renal Consultant that I would switch to HD Dialysis at Skipton Renal Unit and commenced in March of 2018 and continue there today with great results and weight maintained at 81 kg. Since that operation I have not taken any Insulin at all, and my Diabetes has disappeared as if a miracle after 30 years. We now must monitor before, during and after Dialysis Therapy because this process lowers the Blood Sugar substantially. That there is a purpose in everything is evidenced by the fact that I have been able to complete my Autobiography, which I started in 2015, over the past two years in Skipton Dialysis and I am delighted to report that this is complete and published.

Full details are enclosed together with information on "The Neonatal Tree of Life" Project directed by our daughter Dr Michelle Heys Charity 1186748. Each book sale will contribute a minimum £2.00 to the Charity.

I trust that this Article is published as an encouragement to Diabetic and Dialysis patients everywhere and I am willing to give a full presentation for fund raising for the Charity.

If you need to contact me to discuss, please either email or phone as above.

Kind Regards
Bernard Heys MCMI. CWIFM. DipBs.

ADDENDUM C

NKF. Virus Article Book Extract.
NKF Skipton Renal Unit
17.04.2020
Bernard Heys
The Radcliffe
Lad For NKF

Background:
Skipton Renal Unit is a small ten bed satellite unit of Bradford Hospital. For the past two years I have been a Haemodialysis patient at the unit. "My personal thanks to a great team on the front line."

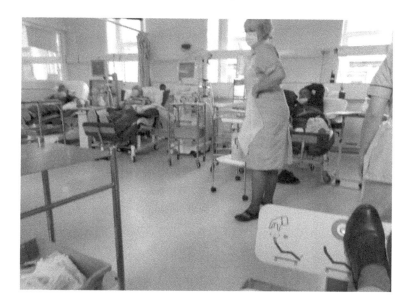

All protected!

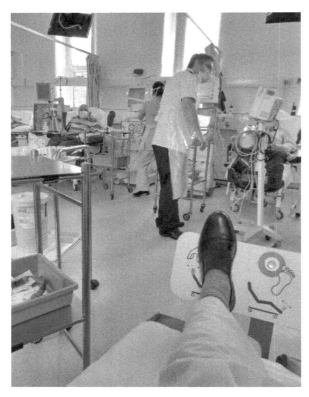

My left foot! Bernard Heys
The Radcliffe Lad

The Unit runs a two-shift system starting at 7am and scheduled to finish at 5pm.

Starting at 7am means that the staff has to be on site at 6.30am in order to organise the setting to work of the various machines which have a different specification and allocate therapy stations for patients with varying therapy for each patient and then allocate each patient to their respective machines. They then prepare and allocate the treatment files and prepare consumables for each patient.

By 7am the scene is set to receive patients.

The unit runs a taxi service for those patients who require this service. Normally the Taxi drivers have also acted as porters to ensure that patients are delivered safely to the unit including patients in wheelchairs.

Also, normally the practice has been to pick up more than one patient and prioritise in accordance with the time that each patient has on dialysis. This varies from as long as 5 hours down to three hours and some have one therapy per week and others three per week.

My personal Feedback:

My main feedback comment to all questionnaires over the past two years has been focused on a lack of adequate funding and resources for this small team.

The second has been related to disconnected communications in the system. IT systems do not talk to each other, and the patient must be the messenger between various Consultants in order to ensure that they have the up to date and correct information as to your medical condition in order to determine any changes in medication and therapy.

Instructions to patients seem to be based on a need-to-know basis but this leads to concern and uncertainty on the part of the patient.

Changes in Practice:

Positive changes in practice due to the Virus have been introduced slowly and piecemeal awaiting advice from higher authority. These changes have added to the workload of all the staff involved and some would argue outside their normal job functions.

Firstly, Taxi drivers and family have been restricted from the unit and the corridors leading to the unit.

Secondly Taxi drivers and family have been restricted from entering the hospital.

Thirdly masks have now been issues to all staff, patients, and Taxi drivers.

Face Mask Barrier protection against Infection. Giving and Receiving the virus.

The mixed messages coming from our Government spokespeople on the efficacy of face wearing masks is totally irresponsible.

Any positive action to erect a barrier against the spread of the virus must be welcomed as a common-sense measure, rather than do nothing. Individuals will want to reduce the risk of them passing on the virus, especially if they have not been tested. People can be positive without showing symptoms.

There is more than adequate evidence the sneeze cloud can fill a room in seconds and travel as far as 10 metres. Each cloud is different and the extent of knowledge of how tenacious the new virus is in attaching itself to the varying size of droplets is minimal so that an arbitrary distance of social separation has been a dangerous assumption especially by dismissing the value of the mask protection.

The Government would be wise to use South Korea as a benchmark especially the preparation they have made since their experience with other coronaviruses such as SARS and MERS, flu, and the common cold.

The Government have stated that they had more than adequate stockpiles of PPE, which has proved to be false, and that they had to establish a distribution chain from scratch.

The Government have failed to give information on the figures required to protect all people at risk, the rate of use and the total to meet needs and quantify the total demand in such an emergency.

Distribution of PPE: Are the Government ignorant of the fact that we have had a Just in Time supply chain for 40 years which can deliver millions of parcels and goods within a day or two and that they had the power to bring this capability into the National Emergency effort.

Investment in Research and Development

They would also be wise to ask the question why investment in research in virulent viruses and tropical diseases by our experts was withdrawn and these experts had to move overseas in order to carry on their research and development programmes.

Taxi drivers are now required to carry only one patient in the back of the car.

Taxi drivers are now required to disinfect the car after each patient journey.

Taxi drivers are not allowed to ferry wheelchair patients into the hospital.

These new requirements add additional burden onto the already stretched nursing staff.

Upon arrival the Taxi driver must phone the duty nurse who then must descend from the unit and take the temperature of the patient outside in the car park.

If this reading is high the patient must be taken home and phone for an ambulance to Bradford. There may be other reasons for a high temperature.

So, without testing for the virus this would increase the risk to the patient who did not have the virus by moving him or her into the higher risk General Hospital environment where there have been positive cases.

If the temperature is normal the patient is allowed into the unit.

Nurses then must act as porters to ferry the wheelchair patients up to the unit.

All this additional work is being carried out whilst the nurses are putting patients onto the machines and thus slows up the process and results in an extended workday for the staff.

"There is then an urgent need to supplement the staff delivering this critical service and therapy with additional volunteers, nurses and porters at Skipton to ease the burden being placed on a very small regular staff."

Personal Therapy:

For myself I have three sessions per week of four hours. Unfortunately, my kidneys do not pass any urine at all which means that the entire fluid intake is retained in my body, and I must be extremely strict as to limiting my daily intake.

In order to start Haemodialysis, I had to have an operation to fit a pair of necklines known as Hudson Lines in order to provide a blood feed and return line to the Dialysis Machine.

These lines must be flushed and cleaned on a regular basis in order to prevent infection but in doing this showering becomes the main difficulty.

My PD Catheter was still fitted in my abdomen but after one year it was decided that I should have another operation to both remove this Catheter and form a Fistula in my wrist.

This would connect the vein to the artery so that when matured would allow the long-term use of needles in the fistula and that replace the neck lines which are susceptible to furring up like a hard water pipe.

My initial sessions on Haemodialysis were not perfect. On several occasions my Blood Pressure dropped so quickly that I started to pass out and lose control over my normal functions.

The challenge then was to find a rate of therapy that I could tolerate without passing out.

The solution came in the form of a highly intelligent Dialysis Machine

working on the principle of "Blood Volume Monitoring" BVM.

This machine monitors, modulates and controls the main bodily parameters that vary through the Therapy. It is systems based and gives feedback signals in order to reduce fluid take off especially if there is a sudden drop in Blood Pressure. It can also advise if more fluid could be taken off.

If this machine is not available, the patient must signal that he or she is in difficulty or the nurse by observation.

(My medical conditions include Diabetes, Dialysis including total loss of kidney function, Unstable Angina, two heart attacks and fitting two Stents, Hypertension, Gout. I am 80 years old but not considered high risk)

The Government did not include Dialysis patients in their high-risk category, and it has taken constant pressure on the NHS to incorporate by my Daughter Dr Michelle Heys.

Bernard Heys
The Radcliffe Lad
19.04.2020

ADDENDUM D

Marketing Autobiography Review Remember Radcliffe Lad
"Know Your Station in Life"
Written in his own words, with a clear purpose, by Bernard Heys
MCMI. CWIFM. DipBs.

He advocates for renewal of his decimated birth town of Radcliffe
Lancashire and for the recognition in both history and the
Industrial Revolution of the RC Community of St Mary's, which
appears to be absent in any recent books on the town.

Following the present debacle over the Referendum, Brexit, and
the complete uncertainty of who holds power in this Country he
also advocates a complete review of our Constitution and Political
System and Reform of outdated Laws for the benefit of all, not
only those who are obsessed with their own wealth and to focus
International efforts to confront the depletion of our resources and
achieve full sustainability and prevention programmes.

The broader purpose of this Autobiography is to inspire a new
generation of Engineering and Construction Apprentices to enjoy
a full and rewarding Career in the most demanding of professional
disciplines.

There is nothing more satisfying than achieving successful project
outcomes.

Autobiography of Bernard (Bernie) Heys
A life story from 10.11.1939 to 10.11.2019
The Radcliffe Lad   A War Baby

Cover Photo HM The Queen by B. Heys.
Back Cover Bobby Moore and Carmel by B. Heys.

Author as a young man

ISBN: 978-1-9133-15-1
ASIN: B0875MCW36
If you need to contact me to discuss, please either email or phone as above.
Bernard Heys MCMI. MWIFM. DipBs.
A 'Print on demand' and self-published project by the Heys family.
Hard Back:
Email for Detailed Flyer or Order: bernieheys@gmail.com
01282843073.
07484246126.

Each of these copies signed by the Author.
E. Book: £4.99
Amazon: www.amazon/remember
Sales of the Hard-Back book will contribute £2.00 to support the Neotree Charity No 1186748.

www.noetree.org

Attention Dr Michelle Heys. michelleheys@gmail.com Written whilst on Haemodialysis in Skipton Renal Unit.

Taking four years to complete due to ill health the main narrative finished on 15.03.2019. The Ides of March.

Embedding of photographs and the Postscript and Epilogue have followed.

Book Contents: 78,125 words, 599 pages, 520 photos.

An Autobiography Covering the period from 10.11.1939 to 10.11.2019 including Family Friends and Fellow Travellers. Written in his own words whilst on Dialysis at Skipton Renal Unit.

He covers the War years and rationing for the first ten years of his life and includes ten years of unnecessary punitive Austerity from 70 to 80 years of age.

'The Extra-ordinary International Life and Career of an Ordinary

Indentured Engineering Apprentice'

From Indentured Aeronautical Engineering Apprentice to Managing Mega Engineering and Construction Projects around the Globe, to Owning a Management Technical and Consultancy Company advising Blue Chip Organisations and Multinational Companies on Organisational Development, Asset and Facilities Management.

A Professional transformational Engineer, Constructor business owner and Management Consultant in the specification, tendering, negotiation, and delivery of 14 mega and 150 medium projects around the world.

From two pound twelve and sixpence per week to one thousand five hundred pounds per day and delivering over £400Bn of present-day value projects and 56 years of high value revenue streams contributions to GDP.

A career of immense challenges and satisfaction, but influenced by incompetent political decisions, and requiring unplanned changes in direction to the career with unexpected results.

A journey through life meeting many well- known people, including Royalty from several Countries, the entertainment world, great cricketers and footballers and football managers.

In addition to recording a life of good fortune the Author expresses dismay at the decimation of his home- town of Radcliffe since incorporation into Bury Metropolitan Borough and the complete failure to recognise the contribution to the development of the Town of St Mary's Community.

Diplomacy and Politics

Including extensive Diplomatic, Political and Cultural differences in Legal systems, Governments and major Engineering and Construction and manufacturing companies in both private and public sectors.

Political commentary and predictions.

The book also covers many of the short-term political decisions that have influenced the direction of travel of our economy and quality of life together with the predictions of "Dark Clouds gathering" following our decision to leave the EU and advocating a complete Constitutional reform of the Political System in the UK, which has demonstrated that it is not fit for purpose of delivering direct democracy at local level to the people of this Country in the 21st Century.

You may have read many of the recent Political and Celebrity Memoirs. You are now invited to read a fascinating autobiography from the opposite spectrum of life.

A book for all the family.

Not a Reality TV Show but the "Real Life Story" of an Indentured Engineering Apprentice and International Mega Projects. You will meet many well-known successful people in your reading journey.

ADDENDUM E

First person experience   21.08.2020

My planned life-long career in the Aerospace Industry was suddenly halted after six years by our Government deciding to cancel our major leading-edge Blue Streak Missile Programme.

This prompted a change in direction of my career and set me on a completely different path and spectacular journey to achieve prominence in the International Engineering and Construction of fourteen mega projects around the world over a period of thirty-one years, working and living with seventy nationalities.

I then established my own Company and for the next twenty-five years delivering Management, Technical and Consultancy Services to Government bodies and Blue-Chip Companies around the Globe.

Several times during my life friends had suggested that I write my life story to record the unusual path I had taken starting as an apprentice with no University education.

After reaching seventy-two years of age, I had to retire through ill health and commenced to outline the purpose and content of my life story. The first purpose was to highlight the removal of the democratic process from my home- town and lack of recognition of my Church and community from any book on the town.

In 2015 however I became seriously ill and spent the next two years on home dialysis, nine hours each night for seven days per week and if the machine mal-functioned I had to phone America for help in the middle of the night.

I then transferred to haemodialysis for three days per week and four hours each therapy; this allowed me to complete my book by my 80th birthday on 10.11.2019.

My Consultant Daughter Dr Michelle Heys then completed the final proof reading, formatting, and Editing and after carrying out due diligence on several printers we visited Book Empire in Leeds to verify the production options and processes and to ensure that our files were compatible with their needs.

We appointed them and submitted our document with separate cover on 10.12.2019 and the first Edition was published locally on 12.01.2020.

Again, after due diligence checks we appointed New Generation to convert the Hard Copy version into the Amazon Kindle version and place on the Kindle platform.

Bernard Heys The Radcliffe Lad

My Station in Life was where-ever the train stopped. Bernard Heys. MCMI. CWIFM. DipBs. bernieheys@gmail.com
01282843073   07484246126
theradcliffelad@gmail.com
Web   www.theradcliffe.co.uk   under construction

ADDENDUM F

Writing projects in progress.

"The Radcliffe Lad Programme of Writing and Publishing"

All works Protected.

1.0 'Manifesto for the People by the People Book'

2.0 'Manifesto TV and Radio Political Programme'

3.0 'Collection of Letters to our Leaders'

4.0 'Dogma Destroys Democracy, Breeds Dictators, Brings Down Parliaments, and Ruins Nations. Book'

5.0 'Health and Care Services in England Book. Concept, The Past, The Present and The Future.'

6.0 The Pendle Papers. 'Legal Dispute Case. In Search of Justice Book'

7.0 'The Kneeling Mea Culpa Manifesto of 2019 Book'

8.0 'My DNA Journey Finding my Station in Life Book.'

9.0 'Martha Through the Ages. Children's Book'

10.0 'Writing and Publishing on Dialysis. Short Story'

11.0 'The Neotree Charity Project Short Story'

Professional Engineers Practical Infection Control' Projects over a 56 Year Career Book.

12.0 Memoir Postscript .28.03.2021

Extract from Remember Radcliffe Lad Know Your Station in Life

Published January 2020

13.03.2019.

I would like to see an informative Political programme, on radio and television, that debates all the key issues, declared in the "Statement of Intent", of all the political parties so that the public are fully informed when asked to vote on the issues that confront our

Nation, not the vague subjective knee jerk pronouncements of our politicians to further their self- interest and legacy in history.

The public to be actively involved rather than our professional commentators and unelected advisors so that we can get some common sense injected into the process based on the quality of life in our so-called wealthy Nation.

To follow up my suggestion of designing a TV programme that is meaningful to and involves the public in the determination of their priorities to be included in a Manifesto for the people, I have registered and recorded a Protection of Work for this idea together with the first draft of a Manifesto Agenda.

The battle now starts for the leadership of the Tory Party but how can it be democratic to have 100,000 "Right Wing" privileged members of our society determining our new Prime Minister, especially with a candidate threatening again to overturn Magna Carta with proroguing Parliament our elected body.

BJ has just repeated the threat not to pay our legally agreed divorce bill of £39billion which is totally irresponsible and could lead to the severing our joint agreements with the EU that have been negotiated over the past 40 years and including those agreements reached during the three-year period since the Referendum result to protect our security and good relations with our European friends.

What kind of example does this set to the country and its citizens working and living within the rule of Law?

Where are the Architects of Austerity, the Referendum and Brexit now but reaping their rewards in kind from the elite supporters of their failed strategies without a glance over their shoulders at the wreckage they have left.

"We look forward with trepidation of a PM who will huff, and he will puff, and he will blow your house down, i.e., the House of Parliament, for his own ends. Beware the Big Bad Wolf in bluff sheep's clothing who has a gait like Napoleon, a nose like Caesar and close-set eyes. After all, would Caesar get into bed with Brutus. BJ has done exactly that with his cat-weasel colleague."

To follow up my suggestion of designing a TV programme that is meaningful to and involves the public in the determination of their priorities to be included in a Manifesto for the people, I have registered and recorded a Protection of Work for this idea together with the first draft of a Manifesto Agenda.

Alexander Boris De Peifel Johnson.03.02.2020

He has not let me down and slipped seamlessly into his Dictators clothes as predicted in my autobiography and adopted his Little Englander posture and believes that he can rule without reference to all the interrelationships that have developed over the past 40 years, especially having outsourced our manufacturing capacity so that we are ill prepared for any unforeseen emergency or global fall out between nations.

We need to rebuild our internal resilience to be able to have a greater self-sufficiency. Our move to low skilled service sector jobs will have a greater negative impact on our economy than most of our European friends who have retained their industrial and manufacturing capacity.

"First President for life of the Republic of the Dis-United Kingdom."

The pied piper of the Tory party pulling all those who signed up to his instruction to conform or die heading for the cliff and extinction. As per my prediction beware the big bad wolf has struck with a vengeance with his Svengali Rasputin companion.

The Dark Clouds have become darker, and our future looks increasingly grim.

If allowed to continue he will isolate the Country from all our friends.

Rumours are that he does not attend or lead the critical Cobra meetings but does his usual disappearing act.

His historic dismissal of the working class as evidenced in his so-called journalistic career and articles written purely to draw attention to himself.

Communities have been stripped of their soul by Central Government removing their same time removing funding to leave the whole Country without any resilience to face Subsidiarity Rights to self- govern but at the future.

PRE-SHIELDING

BERNARD AND CARMEL HEYS

Celebrating 50 Years of Marriage 1970-2020
View of Kelbrook Moors from Robert Hey's House.

With grandchildren in Kelbrook Pre- Lockdown. 10 Millbeck lane Kelbrook.
Darcy, William, Abigail, Martha, Evie Front· Bernard and Carmel Back

Milton Keynes UK
Ingram Content Group UK Ltd.
UKHW010226040624
443357UK00010BA/216/J